You Can Use a Magnifying Glass

By Wiley Blevins

Consultants
David Larwa
National Science Consultant

Nanci R. Vargus, Ed.D.
Assistant Professor of Literacy
University of Indianapolis
Indianapolis, Indiana

Children's Press®
A Division of Scholastic Inc.
New York   Toronto   London   Auckland   Sydney
Mexico City   New Delhi   Hong Kong
Danbury, Connecticut

Designer: Herman Adler Design
Photo Researcher: Caroline Anderson
The photo on the cover shows a boy using a magnifying glass.

Library of Congress Cataloging-in-Publication Data

Blevins, Wiley.
  You can use a magnifying glass / by Wiley Blevins.
      p. cm. – (Rookie read-about science)
Includes index.
Summary: Simple text and photographs describe and illustrate how to use
a magnifying glass.
  ISBN 0-516-22871-4 (lib. bdg.)   0-516-27328-0 (pbk.)
  1. Magnifying glasses–Juvenile literature. [1. Magnifying glasses.]
I. Title. II. Series.
  QC373.M33B55 2003

                              2003003903

CHILDREN'S PRESS, and ROOKIE READ-ABOUT®,
and associated logos are trademarks and or registered trademarks
of Scholastic Library Publishing. SCHOLASTIC and associated logos
are trademarks and or registered trademarks of Scholastic Inc.
1 2 3 4 5 6 7 8 9 10 R 12 11 10 09 08 07 06 05 04 03

What can you see through
a magnifying (MAG-ni-
fye-ng) glass?

Look around with just your eyes. You can see many things.

Some things are too small to see with your eyes alone.

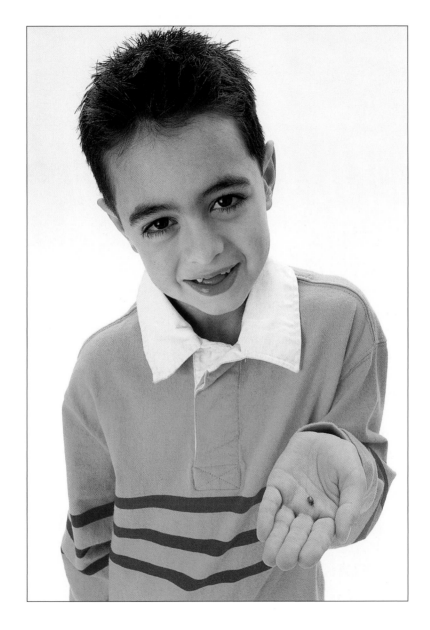

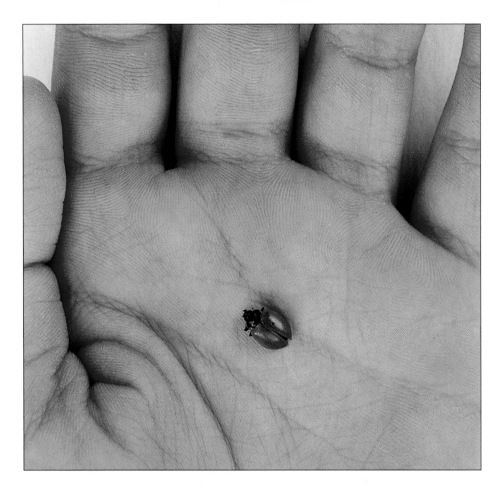

A magnifying glass magnifies,
or makes things bigger.

A magnifying glass can help you see small things.

Look at the back of your hand. It looks smooth.

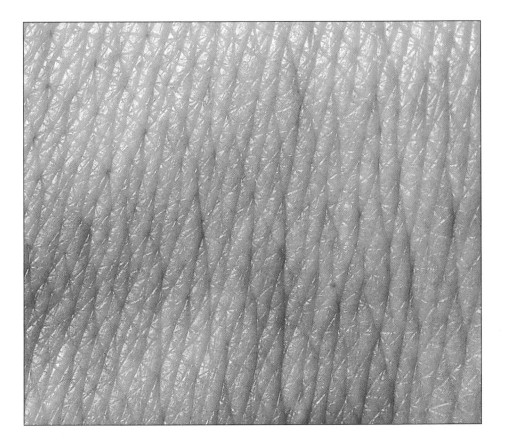

Now look at it through a
magnifying glass. It looks
like it has lots of lines on it.

Look at a dime. It is hard
to see all the details.

Zoom! Now look how big it becomes. What can you see?

This is your tongue.
Look at all those bumps!

This is a butterfly wing.
Look at all the pretty colors.

A magnifying glass is also called a hand lens.

The lens is the glass in the middle. As light hits the lens, the light rays bend. This makes things look bigger.

lens

Scientists (SYE-uhn-tiss)
use magnifying glasses to
study things around them.

They can learn a lot from looking at details.

You can learn a lot
from looking through
magnifying glasses, too.

Look at this fly. Look at
how its eye is made up of
lots of small pieces.

Magnifying glasses can help people do their jobs.

Jewelers use them to look at small stones.

The police use them to find fingerprints. No two fingerprints are alike.

Look at the pattern of lines on a fingerprint. The police can match it to the person who did a crime.

Here is how to look at your fingerprint.

Place one finger on an ink pad. Roll it back and forth. Make sure you get ink all over it. Slowly roll your finger onto a piece of white paper.

Have a friend also make
a fingerprint. Now look
at your fingerprint through
a magnifying glass.

Look at your friend's
fingerprint. How are
they different?

What can you see with
a magnifying glass?

Look again.

29

Words You Know

dime

fingerprint

jeweler

lens

magnifying glass

scientist

31

Index

About the Author

Wiley Blevins is a writer living in New York City. He has written books about such topics as Egypt, slavery, music, and food.

Photo Credits

Photographs © 2003: Corbis Images: 17 (Jack Fields), 21, 30 bottom (Charles O'Rear), 7 (Robert Pickett), 29 (Ariel Skelley), 10, 15, 31 top left; James Levin: cover, 5, 6, 26; Photo Researchers, NY: 11, 30 top left (Ken Cavanagh), 12 (Martin Dohrn/SPL), 13 (Hermann Eisenbeiss), 19 (James H. Robinson); PhotoEdit: 25 (Michael Newman), 3, 8, 31 top right (David Young-Wolff); The Image Works: 16, 31 bottom (Bob Daemmrich), 22, 30 top right (Bonn Sequenze/Imapress); Visuals Unlimited/David Wrobel: 9.